Prayer

CHANGES THINGS

How to Pray Effectively and Move the Hand of God

PETER LENGWE

All Scripture quotations are taken from the New King James Version® (NKJV).

Printed in the United States of America

ISBN:
Softcover: 978-1-972299-45-6
Hardback: 978-1-972299-46-3
eBook: 978-1-972299-44-9

For permission requests, visit and write to the publisher at:

Peter Lengwe | THE BREAD OF LIFE GLOBAL MINISTRIES

PREFACE

"How to Pray Effectively and Move the Hand of God"

Prayer is one of the greatest privileges given to humanity—a divine bridge between the Creator and His creation. Through prayer, the eternal God has given humanity the means to commune with Him, to align with His will, and to invite His power to operate upon the earth. It is not merely a religious exercise or a daily ritual, but a spiritual lifeline that connects heaven and earth.

From the beginning, God desired fellowship with man. In the cool of the day, He walked and talked with Adam in the garden (Genesis 3:8). That intimate communion was the first form of prayer—conversation with God flowing from relationship, not obligation. But when sin entered, that fellowship was broken. Yet in His mercy, God instituted prayer as the means by which man could once again approach Him, speak to Him, and seek His face. Prayer became the way to restore what was lost—a channel through which the heart of man reaches toward the heart of God.

Throughout Scripture, we see men and women who moved heaven by prayer. Abraham interceded for Sodom, and God listened. Hannah wept in the temple, and God gave her a son. Elijah prayed earnestly, and the heavens were shut—and then opened again at his word. Daniel prayed with perseverance and received visions that revealed kingdoms and the end of days. David prayed from a broken and contrite heart, and God called him a man after His own heart. Each one discovered that true prayer is not about eloquence or repetition, but about sincerity, faith, and alignment with the will of God.

But the greatest example of prayer was demonstrated in the life of Jesus Christ. Though He was the Son of God, He never acted independently of His Father. He often withdrew to lonely places to pray, to commune, to align His will with the Father's. From His prayer at the tomb of Lazarus to His high priestly prayer in John 17, and finally to His agonizing prayer in Gethsemane—every word revealed a heart completely surrendered to the will of God. His life teaches us that prayer is not just asking; it is yielding. Not only speaking but also listening. Not demanding our will but desiring His.

This book, "Prayer Changes Things: How to Pray Effectively and Move the Hand of God," is written to teach believers how to pray with understanding, faith, and power. It is a call to return to the altar—to the place of communion and transformation. Through the pages of this book, you will discover what prayer truly is, why God instituted it, and how men and women of faith touched heaven and changed the course of history through it. You will also learn how to position your heart as David did, to pray in such a way that pleases God and brings visible results.

Prayer is not about moving God to do our will—it is about aligning our will with His so that His purposes may be fulfilled through us. When that alignment happens, mountains move, chains break, hearts are healed, and destinies are fulfilled.

May this book ignite in you a deeper hunger for prayer—a hunger not only to speak to God, but to know Him, to walk with Him, and to see His power revealed in your life. For indeed, prayer changes things—but more importantly, prayer changes us.

"The effective, fervent prayer of a righteous man avails much."
(James 5:16, NKJV)

INTRODUCTION

Understanding the Purpose and Power of Prayer

Prayer is the most powerful spiritual force given to man, yet often the most misunderstood and neglected. Many view prayer as a last resort when all else fails, rather than the first place of encounter with the living God. But prayer was never designed to be a backup plan—it was meant to be our daily fellowship, our lifeline, and our partnership with Heaven.

At its core, prayer is communication with God. It is the breath of the spirit, the heartbeat of faith, and the channel through which divine purpose is released upon the earth. True prayer is not simply words spoken; it is communion—it is the spirit of man connecting with the Spirit of God. It is how the created aligns with the Creator to see His will done in time and space.

The Source of Prayer

The source of prayer is God Himself. Prayer was born out of His desire for relationship. In the beginning, before sin entered, man did not need to learn to pray—he walked and talked with God freely. Communication with the Father was natural. But when sin separated man from God, prayer became the bridge of restoration—the means through which man could once again draw near to his Maker.

In Genesis 4:26, it says, "Then men began to call on the name of the LORD." This marks the beginning of prayer as an act of faith, a cry from humanity longing for reconciliation with God. From that moment onward, prayer became the pathway of every soul seeking communion with the Creator.

Prayer, therefore, is not man's invention; it is God's invitation. He is the initiator. When He said in Jeremiah 33:3, "Call to Me, and I will answer you, and show you great and mighty things, which you do not know," He was not commanding us to perform a ritual but inviting us into revelation. Prayer is God saying, "Partner with Me, and I will reveal My heart to you."

Why God Instituted Prayer

God, being Sovereign, could accomplish His will without man. Yet in His divine wisdom, He chose to work through man by means of prayer. Through prayer, man invites the will of God into the earth. Jesus taught us this clearly when He said, "Your kingdom come. Your will be done on earth as it is in heaven." (Matthew 6:10, NKJV).

Prayer, therefore, is not about convincing God to do what we want—it is about coming into agreement with what He has already willed in heaven. It is a divine partnership that releases heavenly authority into earthly situations.

When believers pray according to God's will, they become channels of His power. Heaven responds to the voice of those who are aligned with the Word and heart of God. This is why Jesus said, "If you abide in Me, and My words abide in you, you will ask what you desire, and it shall be done for you." (John 15:7, NKJV).

Prayer as Relationship, Not Ritual

Many pray out of routine, but few pray out of relationship. Prayer is not a performance to impress God—it is an intimate conversation with the Father who already knows what we need before we ask (Matthew 6:8). The purpose of prayer is not information, but transformation. It changes us from the inside out, molding our hearts to reflect His character and our desires to mirror His will.

King David understood this. His prayers were often raw, transparent, and full of emotion. He prayed from the depths of his soul, not merely from his lips. And because his heart was open before God, heaven responded. God called him a man after My own heart (1 Samuel 13:14).

It is the condition of the heart, not the eloquence of words, that moves God. The humble cry of a repentant heart reaches heaven faster than a thousand empty words spoken in pride. Jesus Himself said, "And when you pray, do not use vain repetitions as the heathen do. For they think that they will be heard for their many words." (Matthew 6:7, NKJV).

The Heart of This Book

This book is written to lead believers back to the true essence of prayer—to teach how to pray effectively, fervently, and faithfully, in a way that moves the hand of God. You will learn not only the principles of prayer, but the heart posture that touches God. From the cries of Abraham and Hannah to the intercession of Moses and Daniel, and to the perfect prayer life of Jesus Christ—each chapter will reveal how God responds to hearts that seek Him sincerely.

You will also discover that prayer is not confined to a time or place; it is a lifestyle of communion with God. Prayer can be whispered in a valley of sorrow or shouted in a mountain of victory. Wherever faith is alive, prayer is powerful.

An Invitation to Intimacy

The Spirit of God is calling His people back to the secret place—to the altar of fellowship where fire burns and hearts are changed. God still longs to commune with man as He did in Eden. Through prayer, that fellowship is restored, and His presence becomes tangible once more.

So, as you read this book, do not approach it as information—but as an invitation. Let it draw you deeper into the presence of the One who still says, "Call unto Me." Let it teach you not only how to speak to God, but how to hear His voice. For when your prayer life becomes a place of relationship, your life will become a reflection of His power.

"Now this is the confidence that we have in Him, that if we ask anything according to His will, He hears us."
(1 John 5:14, NKJV)

Table of Contents

CHAPTER ONE:
WHAT IS PRAYER?

Prayer is the breath of the spirit and the language of the heart that seeks God. It is the channel through which man communes with his Creator, not merely through words, but through faith, reverence, and dependence. True prayer is not a duty to be performed—it is a relationship to be nurtured. It is the continual conversation between the soul and God, in which His will becomes known and His power becomes manifest.

In simple terms, prayer is communication with God, but in divine reality, it is much more than that. It is the meeting point of heaven and earth—where mortal man enters the presence of the immortal God to speak, to listen, to yield, and to receive. Prayer is the place where human weakness meets divine strength.

The First Picture of Prayer

Prayer began in the Garden of Eden. Before sin entered, Adam and Eve lived in perfect communion with God. Genesis 3:8 (NKJV) tells us, "And they heard the sound of the Lord God walking in the garden in the cool of the day…" That was fellowship—unbroken communication between God and man. There was no fear, no guilt, and no distance, only pure relationship.

But when sin came, that fellowship was broken. Man hid from God's presence, and distance replaced intimacy. Yet God, in His mercy, still called out, "Adam, where are you?" (Genesis 3:9). Those words reveal the heart of prayer—it is not man searching for God, but God reaching out for man. From that moment on, prayer became the means through which God and man could once again commune.

The Essence of Prayer: Fellowship, Not Formula

The true essence of prayer is not found in formulas, but in fellowship. It is not measured by how long we pray, but by how connected we are to the One we pray to. Prayer is not about speaking many words but about having a heart that listens and responds to the voice of God.

Jesus taught in Matthew 6:7–8 (NKJV),

"And when you pray, do not use vain repetitions as the heathen do. For they think that they will be heard for their many words. Therefore, do not be like them. For your Father knows the things you have need of before you ask Him."

These words reveal the tender heart of the Father. He desires our communion, not our performance. Prayer is not about informing God—it is about transforming us. As we pray, we are drawn closer to Him; our desires are purified, our motives refined, and our hearts aligned with His will.

Prayer as Alignment With God's Will

The power of prayer does not lie in the strength of our voice, but in the alignment of our will with God's will. Jesus said in Matthew 6:10,

"Your kingdom come. Your will be done on earth as it is in heaven."

That is the heart of every true prayer—to see heaven's purpose fulfilled on earth. When we pray according to God's will, heaven responds, and situations change. Prayer is not trying to bend God's arm to agree with us; it is surrendering our will until it agrees with Him.

The Language of Faith

Prayer is also the language of faith. Hebrews 11:6 (NKJV) says, "But without faith it is impossible to please Him, for he who comes to God must believe that He is, and that He is a rewarder of those who diligently seek Him." Every prayer that moves God is birthed in faith—not faith in ourselves, but faith in who God is.

Faith-filled prayer acknowledges God's sovereignty and goodness even before the answer appears. It says, "Father, I trust You," even in uncertainty. True prayer is not measured by how quickly God answers, but by how steadfastly we continue to believe.

The Heart That Moves God

Throughout Scripture, God has always responded to those who sought Him sincerely.

- Hannah's prayer (1 Samuel 1) flowed from anguish, yet it moved heaven and brought forth a prophet.

- Daniel's prayer (Daniel 9–10) was filled with repentance and intercession, and God sent an angel with understanding.

- David's prayers in the Psalms came from a contrite heart, and God called him a man after His own heart.

God listens not to the sound of words, but to the cry of the heart. A broken, humble heart touches heaven more deeply than the loudest declaration. Psalm 34:18 (NKJV) says, "The Lord is near to those who have a broken heart and saves such as have a contrite spirit."

Jesus: The Perfect Example of Prayer

No one modeled prayer more perfectly than Jesus Christ. Though He was the Son of God, He constantly withdrew to pray. Mark 1:35 (NKJV) says, "Now in the morning, having risen a long while before daylight, He went out and departed to a solitary place; and there He prayed."

Jesus' life teaches us that prayer is not an option—it is the oxygen of our spiritual lives. Every miracle He performed, every decision He made, and every act of power flowed from communion with the Father. His life shows that effective prayer begins with relationship, not need.

When Prayer Becomes a Lifestyle

When prayer becomes more than a moment—when it becomes a lifestyle—our lives begin to reflect the power of God. The early church understood this. In Acts 2:42 (NKJV), it says, "And they continued steadfastly in the apostles' doctrine and fellowship, in the breaking of bread, and in prayers."

It was that steadfast devotion to prayer that brought the power of Pentecost and birthed the Church. Likewise, when believers today return to the place of continual prayer, heaven responds with revival.

Reflection and Prayer

Reflection:

Prayer is not about changing God's mind—it's about letting God change our hearts. It is the meeting place between our need and His sufficiency, between our weakness and His strength.

Prayer:

Heavenly Father, thank You for the gift of prayer—my place of refuge, fellowship, and renewal. Teach me to pray not from routine but from relationship. Align my heart with Yours, and let my prayers flow from faith, humility, and love. Draw me closer to You until my desires reflect Your will. In Jesus' name, Amen.

Chapter Two: The Source and Purpose of Prayer

Everything that exists has a source, and that source determines its nature and function. To understand prayer rightly, we must first recognize that its origin is not man's need but God's desire. Prayer began in the heart of God before it was ever expressed by the lips of man. It is not a human idea—it is a divine institution created for fellowship, communication, and partnership between Heaven and earth.

God — The Origin of Prayer

The first act of prayer was not man calling on God, but God calling on man. In Genesis 3:9 (NKJV), after Adam and Eve had sinned, it says,

"Then the Lord God called to Adam and said to him, 'Where are you?'"

This question was not for information but for restoration. God knew where Adam was, yet He called because His heart longed for communion.

That divine call reveals the very foundation of prayer: God always initiates, and man responds.

From the beginning, God's desire was relationship. Prayer is simply the continuation of that relationship in a fallen world. It is God's way of drawing man back to Himself, of keeping the line of fellowship open between Creator and creation.

Prayer — The Fellowship Restored

When sin entered the world, separation came between man and God. But even after man fell, God did not abandon him. Instead, He established prayer as the means through which communication and fellowship could continue. Prayer is therefore the gift of divine access—a way for humanity to approach the throne of grace.

Hebrews 4:16 (NKJV) invites us:

"Let us therefore come boldly to the throne of grace, that we may obtain mercy and find grace to help in time of need."

This verse reveals two beautiful truths:

1. God wants us to come—He invites us.

2. He wants us to receive—He delights to respond.

Thus, prayer is not trying to reach a distant deity; it is responding to a God who has already extended His hand. It is the continuing dialogue of love between a Father and His children.

Why God Instituted Prayer

Although God is sovereign and all-powerful, He chose to involve man in the execution of His will on earth. This partnership is enacted through prayer. It is God's way of granting man the legal right to invite divine intervention into earthly affairs.

When Jesus taught His disciples to pray, He said,

*"Your kingdom come. Your will be done on earth as it is in heaven."
(Matthew 6:10, NKJV)*

That one line reveals the purpose of prayer: to bring heaven's will into earthly reality. Prayer is the spiritual channel that connects God's sovereignty to man's responsibility. Without prayer, heaven's purposes remain unreleased in the realm of men.

This is why God sought intercessors throughout Scripture. In Ezekiel 22:30 (NKJV), He said,

"So, I sought for a man among them who would make a wall, and stand in the gap before Me on behalf of the land, that I should not destroy it; but I found no one."

God's will was to show mercy, but He needed a man to stand in agreement with Him. Prayer becomes that point of agreement—where the will of man and the will of God meet and release divine power.

Prayer Invites God's Dominion

Psalm 115:16 (NKJV) declares,

"The heaven, even the heavens, are the Lord's; but the earth He has given to the children of men."

In His divine order, God entrusted the management of earth to humankind. Therefore, for heaven to intervene, man must invite God through prayer. That is not because God is limited, but because He honors His Word and the authority He gave to man.

When we pray, we are not informing God of our problems—He already knows them. We are, however, inviting His dominion to rule over them. Prayer is the believer's way of saying, "Father, let Your rule and power override this situation." It is the act of transferring control from human hands to divine authority.

The Partnership of Heaven and Earth

Prayer is the link between God's power and man's faith. It is the divine partnership that allows God to move through willing vessels. God does nothing on earth without purpose, and often, His purpose unfolds through the prayers of His people.

Consider Elijah. In 1 Kings 18:1, God told him that He would send rain upon the earth. Yet Elijah still went up to Mount Carmel and prayed earnestly for that rain to fall (1 Kings 18:42–45). God had already spoken His will, but Elijah's prayer released that will into action.

This shows us a vital truth: the promises of God require the prayers of men. God's Word is settled in heaven, but it is established on earth through prayer.

The Relational Purpose of Prayer

While prayer brings results, its greatest purpose is relationship. God does not call us to pray merely so that we can get answers—He calls us to pray so that we can know Him. Every answered prayer should draw us closer to the One who answered.

When Jesus prayed in John 17, His words revealed the true purpose of prayer: intimacy with the Father. He said,

"And this is eternal life, that they may know You, the only true God, and Jesus Christ whom You have sent."
(John 17:3, NKJV)

The ultimate goal of prayer is not power, but presence. It is not to manipulate God's hand, but to know His heart. When you seek His face before you seek His hand, you will find both.

When Prayer Aligns With God's Desire

God always answers prayer that aligns with His purpose. 1 John 5:14–15 (NKJV) assures us :

"Now this is the confidence that we have in Him, that if we ask anything according to His will, He hears us.
And if we know that He hears us, whatever we ask, we know that we have the petitions that we have asked of Him."

To pray effectively, we must therefore learn to pray according to His will. And His will is revealed in His Word. The more we know His Word, the more accurately we can pray.

Summary of Truths

1. Prayer originated with God, not man. It is God's call for fellowship.

2. God instituted prayer so that His will can be manifested on earth through human partnership.

3. Prayer invites God's authority into earthly circumstances.

4. The greatest purpose of prayer is relationship—knowing the heart of God.

5. Prayer aligns man's will with God's will, resulting in divine power and peace.

Reflection and Prayer

Reflection :

The source of prayer is God Himself. He invites us to commune with Him, to partner with Him, and to make His will known on earth. True prayer begins when we respond to His invitation and desire His will above our own.

Prayer:

Father, thank You for calling me into fellowship through prayer. Teach me to see prayer not as a task, but as a privilege to know You and align with Your will. Let my prayers release Your power and accomplish Your purpose in my life and in the earth. I yield my heart, my thoughts, and my desires to You. In Jesus' name, Amen.

Chapter Three:
The Foundation of Effective Prayer

Every lasting structure must be built on a firm foundation. A house without a solid base cannot stand when the storm comes. Likewise, prayer without a foundation cannot stand when trials arise. Many believers pray, but not all see results, because effective prayer is not built on emotion or need—it is built on spiritual principles that align the heart of man with the will of God.

To pray effectively and move the hand of God, one must understand the foundation upon which true prayer stands. These foundations are not mechanical steps but heart postures that please God and invite His presence.

1. Faith – The Substance of Prayer

Faith is the very atmosphere in which prayer lives. Without faith, prayer becomes mere words spoken into the air. Hebrews 11:6 (NKJV) declares:

"But without faith it is impossible to please Him, for he who comes to God must believe that He is, and that He is a rewarder of those who diligently seek Him."

Faith is not just believing that God exists—it is trusting that He listens, He cares, and He will respond according to His Word. The prayer of faith is built on the unshakable confidence that God's promises are true and that His timing is perfect.

When Elijah prayed for rain, he didn't look at the sky; he looked at the Word of the Lord (1 Kings 18:41–45). Though the sky was still clear, Elijah declared, "There is the sound of abundance of rain." That was faith. He prayed with expectation, not doubt.

Faith makes prayer powerful because it connects our words to God's integrity. Faith says, "Even when I do not see, I believe."

2. Humility – The Posture That Draws God Near

Prayer is not a platform to display spiritual pride—it is the altar of surrender. Humility is the foundation upon which the fragrance of prayer rises to God. James 4:6 (NKJV) says,

"God resists the proud but gives grace to the humble."

The proud pray to be seen; the humble pray to be heard. Jesus illustrated this in the parable of the Pharisee and the tax collector (Luke 18:9–14). The Pharisee boasted of his righteousness, but the tax collector bowed his head and said, "God, be merciful to me, a sinner." Jesus said it was the humble man who went home justified.

True humility in prayer acknowledges our dependence on God. It admits, "Lord, without You, I can do nothing." God draws near to such a heart.

3. Obedience – The Key That Opens Heaven

One of the most overlooked foundations of effective prayer is obedience. Prayer is powerful when the heart of the one praying is surrendered to God's commands. 1 John 3:22 (NKJV) declares,

"And whatever we ask we receive from Him, because we keep His commandments and do those things that are pleasing in His sight."

Obedience aligns us with the heart of God. It gives authority to our prayers because our lives agree with His will. Disobedience, on the other hand, creates distance. Isaiah 59:2 says, "Your iniquities have separated you from your God."

When we live in obedience, prayer becomes more than words—it becomes the echo of God's will through a yielded vessel. Jesus Himself modeled this. In John 8:29 (NKJV), He said, "I always do those things that please Him." That obedience gave His prayers unbroken power and authority.

4. Righteousness – The Power of a Clean Heart

James 5:16 (NKJV) declares,

"The effective, fervent prayer of a righteous man avails much."

Righteousness gives power to prayer because sin hinders fellowship. When our hearts are pure before God, our prayers ascend unhindered. This is why David prayed, "Create in me a clean heart, O God, and renew a steadfast spirit within me." (Psalm 51:10).

A righteous heart is not a perfect one, but a repentant one. When we confess and forsake sin, we restore communion with God, and prayer flows freely again. Righteousness is the platform upon which faith stands securely.

5. Persistence – The Spirit That Prevails

Effective prayer is not always answered immediately. Sometimes God allows delay to build endurance and deepen faith. Jesus taught His disciples "that men always ought to pray and not lose heart" (Luke 18:1, NKJV).

In that same chapter, He gave the parable of the persistent widow who kept coming before the unjust judge until he granted her request. Jesus concluded, "And shall God not avenge His own elect who cry out day and night to Him?" (Luke 18:7).

Persistence does not mean trying to persuade God—it means refusing to give up until His will is done. It is the continual knocking that shows faith and determination.

6. The Word of God – The Foundation of Confidence

Effective prayer must be rooted in the Word. God only fulfills His Word, not human wishes. When we pray according to Scripture, we pray in line with His will. Isaiah 55:11 (NKJV) declares,

"So shall My word be that goes forth from My mouth; it shall not return to Me void, but it shall accomplish what I please, and it shall prosper in the thing for which I sent it."

When believers fill their prayers with God's Word, heaven recognizes its own language. Prayer becomes a legal declaration, and God's promises become our petitions.

Jesus Himself used Scripture in prayer. In Gethsemane, His words—"Not My will, but Yours be done"—were the fulfillment of prophecy and submission to God's eternal plan.

7. Love – The Greatest Foundation

Every effective prayer flows out of love—love for God and love for others. Without love, prayer loses its power and becomes self-centered. Paul wrote in 1 Corinthians 13:2 (NKJV),

"Though I have all faith, so that I could remove mountains, but have not love, I am nothing."

Jesus said, "And whenever you stand praying, if you have anything against anyone, forgive him…" (Mark 11:25, NKJV). Forgiveness keeps the heart open for God's answers. Love purifies motives and makes prayer acceptable before the throne.

Examples of a Firm Foundation

- Daniel's prayer life was built on righteousness and faith; he prayed three times daily even in captivity, and heaven responded with visions and angelic revelation.

- Hannah's prayer was filled with humility and persistence; her tears moved heaven and brought forth a prophet.

- Jesus' prayer life stood upon obedience and perfect love; He prayed not for His will, but for the Father's, even unto death.

Each of these examples shows that the foundation of effective prayer is not in the form, but in the heart.

Reflection and Prayer

Reflection :

Prayer that moves God is prayer built on faith, humility, obedience, righteousness, and love. When the foundation is strong, the answers will stand.

Prayer:

Father, I thank You for teaching me the foundation of effective prayer. Establish my heart in faith, humility, and obedience. Cleanse me from all unrighteousness and align me with Your will. Let Your Word dwell richly in me and guide my prayers. May my love for You and for others be the motive behind every request I make. Strengthen me to persist in prayer until Your will is done. In Jesus' name, Amen.

Chapter Four: Different Kinds of Prayer

Prayer is not limited to one form or expression. Just as communication in any relationship varies depending on the situation, prayer takes on different forms according to need, purpose, and divine prompting. Each kind of prayer reveals a unique aspect of our relationship with God and teaches us how to approach Him in faith and sincerity.

The Bible shows us many examples of men and women who prayed in diverse ways—and each time, God responded according to His mercy, faithfulness, and will. Understanding these kinds of prayer helps us grow in intimacy and effectiveness in our walk with Him.

1. The Prayer of Petition – Asking in Faith

The prayer of petition is when we bring our requests before God with faith and confidence in His promises. Philippians 4:6 (NKJV) teaches:

"Be anxious for nothing, but in everything by prayer and supplication, with thanksgiving, let your requests be made known to God."

Petition is not begging—it is presenting a rightful request before the throne of grace based on God's Word.

Example: Hannah's Petition

Hannah's prayer in 1 Samuel 1 was a heartfelt petition. She longed for a child and poured out her soul before the Lord. Her prayer was not loud but sincere. She made a vow to dedicate her son to God if He granted her request. God heard her, and Samuel was born—a prophet who would anoint kings.

Hannah's prayer teaches us that effective petitions are birthed in faith and humility. They come from a heart that trusts God's goodness more than its own desperation.

2. The Prayer of Intercession – Standing in the Gap

Intercession is praying on behalf of others. It is love in action—a reflection of God's own heart. To intercede is to stand between God and another person, city, or nation, pleading for mercy, protection, or blessing.

Example: Abraham's Intercession for Sodom

In Genesis 18, Abraham stood before the Lord and interceded for Sodom, asking God to spare the city if righteous people could be found there. His persistence and compassion moved the heart of God. Though Sodom was eventually destroyed for its wickedness, Lot and his family were rescued because of Abraham's intercession.

Example: Moses' Intercession for Israel

When Israel sinned by worshiping the golden calf, God's anger burned against them. But Moses fell before the Lord and pleaded for mercy. Exodus 32:32 (NKJV) records his powerful words:

"Yet now, if You will forgive their sin—but if not, I pray, blot me out of Your book which You have written."

This is the heart of a true intercessor—one willing to stand in the gap at any cost. God heard Moses' prayer and relented from destroying the nation.

Intercession is a ministry every believer is called to. Jesus Himself is our great Intercessor, ever living to make intercession for us (Hebrews 7:25).

3. The Prayer of Thanksgiving – Remembering God's Goodness

The prayer of thanksgiving is a declaration of gratitude to God for what He has done, is doing, and will do. It keeps the heart humble and faith strong. Gratitude reminds us of God's past faithfulness and stirs confidence for the future.

1 Thessalonians 5 :18 (NKJV) says,

"In everything give thanks; for this is the will of God in Christ Jesus for you."

Example: King David's Thanksgiving

David's psalms are filled with prayers of thanksgiving. He said, "Bless the Lord, O my soul, and forget not all His benefits" (Psalm 103:2). Even in hardship, David chose to thank God, knowing His mercy endures forever.

Example: Jesus' Thanksgiving Before the Miracle

Before multiplying the loaves and fish, Jesus gave thanks (John 6:11). Thanksgiving preceded the miracle. Gratitude opens the door for God's power to work, because it expresses faith that He has already made provision.

A thankful heart keeps the believer in constant communion with God and shuts the door to fear and complaint.

4. The Prayer of Repentance – Returning to God

Repentance is not only turning from sin—it is turning to God. The prayer of repentance restores broken fellowship and renews the heart. God never despises a repentant spirit. Psalm 51:17 (NKJV) declares,

"The sacrifices of God are a broken spirit, a broken and a contrite heart—these, O God, You will not despise."

Example: David's Prayer of Repentance

After his sin with Bathsheba, David prayed from the depths of his heart:

"Create in me a clean heart, O God, and renew a steadfast spirit within me."
(Psalm 51:10, NKJV)

He did not excuse his sin; he confessed it openly. God forgave him and restored him.

Example: The Prodigal Son's Return

In Luke 15, the prodigal son's prayer of repentance began in his heart before he ever spoke it: "I will arise and go to my father." His humility brought restoration, showing that repentance is not weakness but the doorway to mercy.

5. The Prayer of Surrender – Yielding to God's Will

Surrender is the highest form of prayer because it requires trust beyond understanding. It is the place where faith and obedience meet. Jesus demonstrated this kind of prayer in the Garden of Gethsemane.

Example: Jesus' Prayer in Gethsemane

In Matthew 26:39 (NKJV), Jesus prayed,

"O My Father, if it is possible, let this cup pass from Me; nevertheless, not as I will, but as You will."

This was not a prayer of weakness but of divine strength. Jesus' surrender opened the way for salvation. When we pray in surrender, we release control and allow God's perfect will to unfold.

True victory in prayer is not when we get what we want—it is when we embrace what God wants.

6. The Prayer of Agreement – Unity in Faith

The prayer of agreement is powerful because it unites believers in faith toward a common request. Jesus said in Matthew 18:19 (NKJV),

"Again, I say to you that if two of you agree on earth concerning anything that they ask, it will be done for them by My Father in heaven."

Example: The Church Praying for Peter

In Acts 12:5, the early church prayed fervently for Peter while he was in prison. God responded by sending an angel to set him free. Unity in prayer releases multiplied power because agreement amplifies faith.

When believers come together in one accord—seeking God's will and not their own—the heavens open.

7. The Prayer of Worship – Adoration and Reverence

Worship is prayer without request. It is communion expressed through love, awe, and adoration. It exalts who God is, not just what He does.

John 4:23–24 (NKJV) says,

"But the hour is coming, and now is, when the true worshipers will worship the Father in spirit and truth; for the Father is seeking such to worship Him."

Example: Jehoshaphat's Worship Before Victory

When Judah faced a vast army, King Jehoshaphat bowed before God and worshiped. The singers went before the army, praising the Lord, and the enemies destroyed each other (2 Chronicles 20:21–22). Worship turned a battlefield into a place of victory.

When worship becomes our prayer, battles are won without swords, because God Himself fights for those who honor Him.

The Response of God to Prayer

In every kind of prayer—petition, intercession, thanksgiving, repentance, surrender, agreement, or worship—God's response is consistent: He listens.

Psalm 65:2 calls Him "You who hear prayer." He hears not because of our eloquence, but because of His covenant love.

Every sincere prayer finds its way to the throne of grace. Revelation 5:8 describes the prayers of the saints as golden bowls full of incense before God. No prayer offered in faith is ever wasted.

Reflection and Prayer

Reflection :

Prayer takes many forms, but all true prayer flows from the heart and leads us closer to God. Whether in thanksgiving, intercession, or surrender, each prayer draws us deeper into His presence.

Prayer:

Father, thank You for teaching me the many ways to communicate with You. Help me to pray with understanding and sincerity in every season. Teach me to intercede for others, to give thanks continually, to repent humbly, and to surrender fully to Your will. Let my prayers rise before You as incense and move Your heart to act in righteousness and mercy. In Jesus' name, Amen.

Chapter Five: The Prayer Life of Jesus Christ

The life of Jesus Christ was marked by power, authority, and compassion — but at the center of it all was prayer. Every miracle He performed, every decision He made, and every word He spoke flowed from His intimate fellowship with the Father. His entire ministry was birthed, sustained, and completed in prayer.

Though Jesus was the Son of God, He lived on earth as the Son of Man — fully dependent on the Father and the Holy Spirit. He never acted independently of heaven. Prayer was His lifeline, His source of direction, strength, and communion. If Jesus — perfect, sinless, and divine — needed to pray, how much more do we?

Prayer Was the Heartbeat of His Life

From the beginning of His ministry, Jesus demonstrated the importance of personal prayer.

Mark 1:35 (NKJV) records:

"Now in the morning, having risen a long while before daylight, He went out and departed to a solitary place; and there He prayed."

Before the crowds, before the miracles, and before the day began — Jesus met with the Father. His priority was not ministry, but intimacy. His secret place was His source of public power.

This pattern is seen repeatedly throughout the Gospels. Luke 5:16 (NKJV) says,

"So, He Himself often withdrew into the wilderness and prayed."

The word often shows consistency. Jesus didn't pray occasionally — He lived in continual fellowship. Prayer for Him was not a duty but a delight, not a ritual but a relationship.

Prayer Before Every Major Decision

Jesus never made a decision without first seeking the Father's will. Before choosing the twelve apostles, Luke 6:12 (NKJV) says,

"Now it came to pass in those days that He went out to the mountain to pray and continued all night in prayer to God."

Imagine the Son of God spending the entire night in communion with the Father before selecting His disciples. That reveals a powerful truth: direction comes from intimacy.

When we learn to pray before we act, we allow God to align our choices with His perfect plan. Jesus' all-night prayer teaches us that the will of God is discovered in the place of prayer, not assumption.

Prayer as the Source of Power

Before Jesus began His public ministry, He prayed. In Luke 3:21–22 (NKJV), we read that as He prayed during His baptism, "heaven was opened, and the Holy Spirit descended in bodily form like a dove upon Him."

Prayer opens heaven. It invites the Holy Spirit to descend and empower us. Every time Jesus prayed, divine power followed. He prayed before feeding the multitudes, before raising Lazarus, before healing the sick, and even before facing the cross.

In John 11:41–42 (NKJV), at the tomb of Lazarus, He lifted His eyes and said,

"Father, I thank You that You have heard Me. And I know that You always hear Me."

This simple yet profound statement reveals the unbroken confidence He had in His Father's faithfulness. He didn't pray to be heard; He prayed because He was heard.

Prayer of Intercession for Others

The prayer life of Jesus was not self-centered. He continually interceded for others — for His disciples, for the sick, for the lost, and even for His enemies.

In John 17, known as the "High Priestly Prayer," Jesus prayed passionately for those the Father had given Him:

"I do not pray for these alone, but also for those who will believe in Me through their word."
(John 17:20, NKJV)

This means that over two thousand years ago, Jesus prayed for you — for every believer who would come to faith through the Gospel. His intercession spans generations.

Even on the cross, His final prayers were for others: "Father, forgive them, for they do not know what they do." (Luke 23:34, NKJV). Such love is divine — a heart that intercedes even in suffering.

And today, His ministry of prayer continues. Hebrews 7:25 (NKJV) declares,

"He always lives to make intercession for them."

The same Jesus who prayed on earth still intercedes in heaven for His people.

Prayer of Thanksgiving

Gratitude was central to the prayers of Jesus. He often gave thanks before performing miracles. In John 6:11, He took the loaves and fish, "and when He had given thanks, He distributed them."

Likewise, before raising Lazarus, He said, "Father, I thank You that You have heard Me." Thanksgiving preceded the manifestation of power. Jesus teaches us that gratitude in prayer demonstrates trust — it declares that God has already made provision.

Thanksgiving transforms prayer from anxiety to assurance, from fear to faith.

Prayer of Surrender in Gethsemane

The most powerful and emotional prayer of Jesus was in the Garden of Gethsemane. It reveals the full surrender of His human will to the Father's divine plan. Matthew 26:39 (NKJV) records,

"He went a little farther and fell on His face, and prayed, saying, 'O My Father, if it is possible, let this cup pass from Me; nevertheless, not as I will, but as You will.'"

In this moment, Jesus experienced the weight of humanity's sin and the agony of separation. Yet His love for the Father and for us triumphed. His submission in prayer became the turning point of redemption.

Gethsemane teaches us that the highest form of prayer is surrender — yielding to God even when His will leads through suffering. The answer to

Jesus' prayer was not deliverance, but divine strength to fulfill the Father's purpose. Luke 22:43 (NKJV) says, "Then an angel appeared to Him from heaven, strengthening Him."

When we pray as Jesus did, saying, "Not my will, but Yours be done," heaven responds with strength, grace, and peace to carry out God's will.

Lessons from the Prayer Life of Jesus

1. He prayed continually. Prayer was His lifestyle, not an emergency response.

2. He prayed privately. His greatest victories were won in solitude.

3. He prayed before decisions. Guidance came through communion.

4. He prayed for others. His prayers flowed from love and compassion.

5. He prayed with thanksgiving. Gratitude preceded every miracle.

6. He prayed in surrender. His will was always aligned with the Father's.

If we follow His example, our prayer lives will shift from ritual to relationship and from striving to resting in God's will.

Reflection and Prayer

Reflection :

Jesus' life was a continual dialogue with the Father. Every prayer revealed dependence, obedience, and love. To pray like Jesus is to seek the Father's will above our own and to remain in constant communion with Him.

Prayer:

Heavenly Father, thank You for the perfect example of prayer shown through Your Son, Jesus Christ. Teach me to seek You early and often, to pray before decisions, to intercede for others, and to walk in gratitude and surrender. Let my prayer life reflect the heart of Jesus — humble, faithful, and full of love. Strengthen me to say in every season, "Not my will, but Yours be done." In Jesus' name, Amen.

Chapter Six:
How to Pray to Touch God's Heart

The greatest secret of effective prayer is not found in eloquence or length, but in the condition of the heart. God is not moved by the abundance of words but by the sincerity of spirit. The prayer that touches heaven begins in the heart that is humble, broken, and full of love for God.

Many can pray loudly, but few pray deeply. True prayer flows not from the lips, but from the soul that yearns for fellowship with its Maker. When the heart is right before God, even the simplest whisper becomes powerful.

God Looks at the Heart

When the prophet Samuel went to anoint a king among Jesse's sons, he looked at the outward appearance. But God corrected him:

"For the Lord does not see as man sees; for man looks at the outward appearance, but the Lord looks at the heart."
(1 Samuel 16:7, NKJV)

This truth also governs prayer. God does not measure our words—He measures our hearts. A proud heart cannot move God, but a contrite heart invites His presence. Psalm 51:17 (NKJV) declares,

"The sacrifices of God are a broken spirit, a broken and a contrite heart—these, O God, You will not despise."

David — A Man After God's Own Heart

King David was not perfect, yet God called him "a man after My own heart." What made David different from others was his heart posture before God.

David prayed with passion, repentance, and honesty. He never tried to hide his failures; he poured them out before God. In Psalm 62:8 (NKJV) he wrote,

"Trust in Him at all times, you people; pour out your heart before Him; God is a refuge for us."

David's secret was transparency. His prayers revealed a heart that longed for God more than His blessings. Whether in victory or in failure, David sought the presence of the Lord more than anything else.

When he sinned, he did not defend himself—he repented. When he succeeded, he gave glory to God. When he was pursued by enemies, he cried out in faith. And when he was restored, he sang songs of thanksgiving. Every stage of David's life was marked by prayer.

This teaches us that the prayer that touches God's heart is the prayer of sincerity—when nothing is hidden, and all is surrendered.

The Posture of a Heart That Moves God

1. Humility – The heart that bows before God stands strong before men.

- *"Humble yourselves in the sight of the Lord, and He will lift you up." (James 4:10, NKJV)*
  Humility admits dependence on God. It says, "Lord, without You I can do nothing."

2. Repentance – The heart that quickly repents stays in fellowship.

- *David's prayer in Psalm 51 reveals a deep sorrow for sin and a longing for restoration. God responds swiftly to the repentant heart.*

3. Faith – The heart that believes receives.

- *Jesus said, "Whatever things you ask when you pray, believe that you receive them, and you will have them." (Mark 11:24, NKJV)*
  Faith-filled prayer moves mountains because it is rooted in trust.

4. Obedience – The heart that obeys delights God.

- *"And whatever we ask we receive from Him, because we keep His commandments." (1 John 3:22, NKJV)*
  When we walk in obedience, our prayers align with His will.

5. Love – The heart of prayer must beat with love.

- *Prayer without love becomes ritual, but prayer born of love becomes worship. Jesus said, "If you love Me, keep My commandments." (John 14:15, NKJV)*

Jesus — The Perfect Example of a Heart That Touched God

Jesus' prayers always moved the Father because His heart was perfectly aligned with God's will. In John 11:41–42, before raising Lazarus, He prayed,

"Father, I thank You that You have heard Me. And I know that You always hear Me."

He was heard because His heart was pure and His motive was love. Even in His greatest agony in Gethsemane, His prayer was not self-centered but surrendered:

"Nevertheless, not My will, but Yours, be done." (Luke 22:42, NKJV)

This is the ultimate expression of a heart that touches God—a heart willing to yield, even when it costs everything.

How to Position Your Heart in Prayer

- Be Honest: Speak openly to God. He already knows your thoughts.

- Be Reverent: Approach Him with awe and respect.

- Be Thankful: Gratitude opens the gates of His presence.

- Be Persistent: Don't give up; keep trusting.

- Be Surrendered: Let God's will outweigh your own desires.

When the heart is rightly positioned, the words matter little—the Spirit intercedes through groanings too deep for words (Romans 8:26).

The Prayer That Moved Heaven

In Luke 18:13, Jesus told of a tax collector who simply prayed, "God, be merciful to me a sinner." That short prayer touched heaven more than the self-righteous words of the Pharisee beside him.

Why? Because the heart behind it was humble, honest, and repentant. The man went home justified before God.

Prayer that moves the heart of God is not measured in minutes but in motive. It is not about the volume of words, but the depth of surrender.

The Result of a Heart That Touches God

When the heart aligns with God, prayer becomes powerful. The believer begins to experience divine favor, guidance, and peace. Philippians 4:6–7 (NKJV) assures us :

"Be anxious for nothing, but in everything by prayer and supplication, with thanksgiving, let your requests be made known to God. and the peace of God, which surpasses all understanding, will guard your hearts and minds through Christ Jesus."

The greatest answer to prayer is not always a change in circumstance, but a transformation in the heart.

Reflection and Prayer

Reflection :

The prayer that touches God's heart flows from humility, love, faith, and surrender. When our motives are pure and our hearts are open, God draws near and reveals His favor.

Prayer:

Father, I desire to know You and to pray from a heart that pleases You. Remove pride, selfishness, and fear from within me. Create in me a clean heart and renew a steadfast spirit. Teach me to pray with sincerity and to seek Your will more than anything else. Let my words and desires be shaped by Your Word and Spirit. May my prayers rise before You as a sweet aroma, touching Your heart as David's did. In Jesus' name, Amen.

Chapter Seven: Obstacles to Answered Prayer

Every believer desire to see their prayers answered, yet many struggle with silence from heaven. God is faithful to hear and respond, but there are times when certain barriers stand between the prayer and the answer. These obstacles are not signs of God's unwillingness to act, but signals that something must be corrected or surrendered for His power to flow freely.

God's Word makes it clear that He hears the righteous cry, but He also reveals conditions that can hinder prayer. Understanding these helps us remove what blocks our communion with Him so that nothing separates us from His presence or delays His promises.

1. Unconfessed Sin

Sin is the greatest barrier between man and God. Isaiah 59:2 (NKJV) says,

"But your iniquities have separated you from your God; and your sins have hidden His face from you, so that He will not hear."

Sin interrupts fellowship and silences effective prayer. It is not that God cannot hear—He chooses not to respond until repentance restores relationship.

David understood this clearly. After his fall, he prayed, "If I regard iniquity in my heart, the Lord will not hear." (Psalm 66:18, NKJV). But when he confessed, God forgave and restored him.

The solution to this obstacle is repentance. 1 John 1:9 (NKJV) promises,

"If we confess our sins, He is faithful and just to forgive us our sins and to cleanse us from all unrighteousness."

Confession reopens the line of communication with God and restores intimacy.

2. Unforgiveness

Few things block prayer more effectively than an unforgiving heart. Jesus said plainly,

"And whenever you stand praying, if you have anything against anyone, forgive him, that your Father in heaven may also forgive you your trespasses."
(Mark 11:25, NKJV)

Forgiveness is not optional—it is essential. An unforgiving spirit imprisons the one who prays. When we hold grudges, we close our hearts to the mercy of God.

Stephen, even while being stoned, prayed, "Lord, do not charge them with this sin." (Acts 7:60). His prayer of forgiveness mirrored Jesus' words on the cross. Forgiveness liberates the soul and releases God's power to work both in us and through us.

To pray effectively, we must forgive as we have been forgiven.

3. Doubt and Unbelief

Doubt poisons the roots of prayer. It questions God's faithfulness and cripples faith before it bears fruit. James 1:6–7 (NKJV) warns,

"But let him ask in faith, with no doubting, for he who doubts is like a wave of the sea driven and tossed by the wind. For let not that man suppose that he will receive anything from the Lord."

Faith anchors prayer in God's character. When we doubt, we focus on the problem rather than the promise. Unbelief short-circuits divine response because it dishonors God's Word.

The cure for doubt is the Word of God, for "faith comes by hearing, and hearing by the word of God." (Romans 10:17). Filling our hearts with Scripture builds confidence that what God has promised, He will perform.

4. Wrong Motives

Prayer that is self-centered or flesh-driven cannot move heaven. James 4:3 (NKJV) says,

"You ask and do not receive, because you ask amiss, that you may spend it on your pleasures."

God examines motives before He answers petitions. He is not moved by selfish ambition, but by kingdom purpose. Jesus taught us to pray, "Your kingdom come, Your will be done on earth as it is in heaven." (Matthew 6:10).

When our desires are purified and aligned with God's heart, our prayers become effective. A prayer prayed from love, obedience, and compassion always gets heaven's attention.

5. Disobedience and Rebellion

Prayer without obedience is empty sound. God delights in those who hear His Word and keep it. Proverbs 28:9 (NKJV) warns,

"One who turns away his ear from hearing the law, even his prayer is an abomination."

To pray effectively, our lives must reflect submission to God's authority. Jesus said, "If you love Me, keep My commandments." (John 14:15, NKJV). Obedience is the fragrance that makes prayer acceptable before the throne.

When we walk in rebellion or compromise, we block our own blessings. But when we repent and obey, the heavens open again.

6. Prayerlessness and Neglect

Sometimes the obstacle is not sin or doubt but simply neglect. Many believers grow weary or distracted and cease to pray. Yet Jesus said, "Men always ought to pray and not lose heart." (Luke 18:1, NKJV).

When prayer ceases, spiritual strength fades. Neglect closes the channel of divine communication, allowing worry and weakness to take root.

God's instruction in 1 Thessalonians 5 :17 is clear : "Pray without ceasing." A consistent prayer life keeps the heart sensitive to God's voice and shields the soul from temptation.

To overcome neglect, prayer must become a lifestyle, not a last resort.

7. Lack of Compassion or Mercy

Another hindrance to answered prayer is hardness of heart toward others. Proverbs 21:13 (NKJV) warns,

"Whoever shuts his ears to the cry of the poor will also cry himself and not be heard."

Prayer that pleases God flows from a merciful heart. When we care for what God cares for—the lost, the suffering, the broken—our prayers align with His compassion.

Jesus wept over Jerusalem and prayed for those who persecuted Him. When we walk in mercy, our prayers carry divine fragrance before the throne.

8. Marital Discord and Dishonor

For those who are married, disharmony can block prayer. 1 Peter 3:7 (NKJV) says,

"Husbands, likewise, dwell with them with understanding, giving honor to the wife... that your prayers may not be hindered."

Prayer is hindered when there is strife in the home, for God honors unity. Whether husband or wife, both must walk in love, honor, and humility for heaven's blessing to flow freely.

Unity invites divine favor; discord invites delay.

9. Lack of Persistence

Some prayers are hindered not because of sin, but because the believer gives up too soon. Jesus told the parable of the persistent widow (Luke 18:1–8) to show that faith must persevere.

Delay is not denial. God often uses waiting seasons to strengthen faith, refine motives, and prepare the heart for greater blessing. Daniel prayed for twenty-one days before the angel appeared with his answer, saying, "From the first day that you set your heart to understand... your words were heard." (Daniel 10:12, NKJV).

Persistence demonstrates trust in God's timing. The prayer that refuses to quit will eventually see breakthrough.

How to Remove These Obstacles

1. Repent quickly when the Spirit convicts you.

2. Forgive freely as you have been forgiven.

3. Pray in faith, not fear, or doubt.

4. Purify your motives through the Word.

5. Obey God's Word even in insignificant things.

6. Be consistent in prayer; make it your lifestyle.

7. Walk in mercy and compassion toward others.

8. Live in peace and honor with those around you.

9. Be patient and persistent until the answer comes.

When these hindrances are removed, the channel of communication opens wide, and the believer begins to experience answered prayer and divine peace.

Reflection and Prayer

Reflection :

Prayer is powerful, but purity of heart and faith in God make it effective. Removing the obstacles clears the way for divine response. When nothing stands between you and God, heaven moves on your behalf.

Prayer:

Heavenly Father, thank You for showing me the things that hinder prayer. Search my heart and remove every obstacle that blocks Your presence. Forgive me for any sin, doubt, or unforgiveness. Purify my motives and teach me to walk in obedience, love, and mercy. Strengthen my faith to persist until Your will is done. Let nothing separate me from Your fellowship or hinder Your answers. In Jesus' name, Amen.

Chapter Eight:
The Power of Persistent
and Collective Prayer

Prayer is not only a personal conversation with God but also a divine weapon of perseverance and unity. Some victories are won in a moment of faith, but others require persistence — the kind of prayer that refuses to quit until heaven responds. Likewise, some breakthroughs are released not through individual prayer alone but through collective agreement when the body of Christ unites in faith and intercession.

Persistent prayer demonstrates faith that does not faint; collective prayer releases multiplied power that moves mountains. Together, they form a spiritual force that shakes the earth and opens the heavens.

1. The Power of Persistent Prayer

Jesus taught persistence as a mark of true faith. In Luke 18:1 (NKJV), He said,

"Men always ought to pray and not lose heart."

He followed this with the parable of the persistent widow who kept coming before an unjust judge, pleading for justice. Though the judge had no fear of God or regard for man, her persistence compelled him to act. Jesus concluded,

"And shall God not avenge His own elect who cry out day and night to Him, though He bears long with them?" (Luke 18:7, NKJV).

Persistence in prayer is not about trying to convince God; it is about proving our trust in Him. It refines our faith, purifies our motives, and strengthens our endurance.

God often delays not because He is unwilling but because He is preparing us for the answer. Delay builds spiritual maturity. When we keep praying, even in silence, heaven takes notice.

2. Daniel's Example of Persevering Prayer

Daniel's persistence is one of the greatest examples of unwavering faith in Scripture. In Daniel 10, he prayed and fasted for twenty-one days without receiving an answer. Yet when the angel finally appeared, he said,

"From the first day that you set your heart to understand, and to humble yourself before your God, your words were heard." (Daniel 10:12, NKJV).

The answer was released from the first day, but spiritual warfare delayed its arrival. Daniel's perseverance broke through that resistance.

This teaches us that persistent prayer is not wasted prayer. Even when we see no visible result, something is happening in the unseen realm. Prayer never dies; it accumulates power until the breakthrough manifests.

3. Elijah — A Picture of Fervent and Persistent Faith

Elijah's prayer life demonstrates the link between persistence and divine manifestation. In 1 Kings 18, after three and a half years of drought, he went up to Mount Carmel to pray for rain. He bowed down to the ground and prayed — not once, but seven times.

Each time his servant returned with the report, "There is nothing." But Elijah refused to give up. On the seventh time, the servant saw a small cloud like a man's hand rising from the sea. That small sign was enough for Elijah to declare, "Prepare your chariot, and go down before the rain stops you!"

Faith persisted until the heavens opened. Persistence brings the invisible into the visible. Elijah's example teaches us that breakthrough comes to those who refuse to stop praying.

4. Jesus' Teaching on Persistent Asking

In Luke 11:5–10, Jesus gave the parable of the friend at midnight who persistently knocked on his neighbor's door asking for bread. Though the man was initially reluctant, he eventually responded because of his friend's persistence.

Jesus used this story to reveal the Father's heart:

"So, I say to you, ask, and it will be given to you; seek, and you will find; knock, and it will be opened to you." (Luke 11:9, NKJV).

The verbs ask, seek, knock imply continuous action — keep asking, keep seeking, keep knocking. Prayer that perseveres in faith will always open doors.

5. The Power of Collective Prayer

While persistence strengthens the individual, unity multiplies the power of prayer. Jesus declared in Matthew 18:19–20 (NKJV),

"If two of you agree on earth concerning anything that they ask, it will be done for them by My Father in heaven. For where two or three are gathered together in My name, I am there in the midst of them."

When believers pray in agreement, the presence of Jesus Himself joins that prayer. Collective prayer unites hearts, aligns faith, and draws divine power into situations.

6. The Early Church and the Power of United Intercession

The early Church understood the power of praying together. When Peter was imprisoned by Herod, the believers gathered in one accord to intercede for him. Acts 12:5 (NKJV) says,

"Peter was therefore kept in prison, but constant prayer was offered to God for him by the church."

God responded immediately. An angel entered the prison, broke his chains, and led him out to freedom. The prayer of the Church moved heaven and overturned an earthly decree.

This is the power of corporate intercession — when God's people unite with one voice and one purpose, heaven moves in response.

Collective prayer also birthed revival at Pentecost. Acts 2:1–2 (NKJV) records,

"When the Day of Pentecost had fully come, they were all with one accord in one place. And suddenly there came a sound from heaven, as of a rushing mighty wind..."

Unity invites suddenlies — divine visitations that change everything.

7. The Secret of Agreement in Prayer

Amos 3:3 (NKJV) asks,

"Can two walk together, unless they are agreed?"

Agreement in prayer is more than saying the same words—it means unity in spirit, motive, and faith. When hearts are aligned with God and each other, there is exponential power.

One can chase a thousand, but two can put ten thousand to flight (Deuteronomy 32:30). That is the divine equation of agreement. Collective prayer multiplies spiritual force against the powers of darkness.

8. Modern Lessons for the Church

Today, the Church must rediscover the strength of united, persistent prayer. The world grows darker, but heaven's light shines brighter through praying believers. Revival, deliverance, and transformation will never come through strategy alone, but through prayer that is fervent and united.

When the Church prays together with one heart — as in the book of Acts — the Holy Spirit moves, and the kingdom of God advances.

Persistent prayer builds faith; collective prayer builds community. Together, they make the Church unstoppable.

Reflection and Prayer

Reflection :

Persistent prayer reveals faith that endures; collective prayer reveals unity that conquers. When believers pray continually and in one accord, mountains move, doors open, and God's will is done on earth as it is in heaven.

Prayer:

Father, thank You for the power of persistent and collective prayer. Teach me to keep praying when answers seem delayed and to join hands with others in faith. Unite Your Church in love and purpose, that our prayers may release Your power across nations. Help me never to grow weary, but to stand firm until Your promises manifest. Let our prayers shake the heavens and bring glory to Your name. In Jesus' name, Amen.

Chapter Nine:
The Holy Spirit and Prayer

Every true prayer that reaches the throne of God is inspired and sustained by the Holy Spirit. Without Him, prayer becomes effort; with Him, it becomes power. The Holy Spirit is not only the Comforter but also the Intercessor within us — the One who gives voice to our spirit, aligning our prayers with the perfect will of the Father.

Through Him, prayer moves from human weakness to divine strength, from words of earth to utterances of heaven.

The Promise of Power and the Birth of the Church

Before His ascension, Jesus instructed His disciples to wait in Jerusalem until they were "endued with power from on high." (Luke 24:49, NKJV). This power was the Holy Spirit — the promised Comforter who would not only dwell with them but live within them.

In Acts 1:8 (NKJV), Jesus declared,

"But you shall receive power when the Holy Spirit has come upon you; and you shall be witnesses to Me in Jerusalem, and in all Judea and Samaria, and to the end of the earth."

They waited, and on the Day of Pentecost, the promise was fulfilled. Acts 2:1–4 (NKJV) records:

"When the Day of Pentecost had fully come, they were all with one accord in one place.
And suddenly there came a sound from heaven, as of a rushing mighty wind, and it filled the whole house where they were sitting.
Then there appeared to them divided tongues, as of fire, and one sat upon each of them.
And they were all filled with the Holy Spirit and began to speak with other tongues, as the Spirit gave them utterance."

This was not merely an event — it was the beginning of a new era. The same disciples who once feared and hid now prayed boldly and spoke in heavenly languages, empowered by the Spirit. Pentecost changed everything.

The Baptism of the Holy Spirit and Prayer in a New Tongue

At Pentecost, believers were baptized in the Holy Spirit — not only to testify of Christ but to commune with God in a new dimension of prayer. Speaking in tongues, or praying in the Spirit, was a divine gift that enabled them to pray beyond the limits of human language and understanding.

Paul explained this mystery in 1 Corinthians 14:14–15 (NKJV):

"For if I pray in a tongue, my spirit prays, but my understanding is unfruitful.
What is the conclusion then? I will pray with the spirit, and I will also pray with the understanding."

Praying in the Spirit is the Holy Spirit praying through us — expressing the deep desires and burdens of the heart that words cannot capture. It is communication that flows directly from the spirit of man to the Spirit of God.

This kind of prayer strengthens, edifies, and refreshes the believer. Jude 20 (NKJV) says,

"But you, beloved, building yourselves up on your most holy faith, praying in the Holy Spirit."

When we pray in tongues, our faith is stirred, our spiritual strength renewed, and our intimacy with God deepened.

The Holy Spirit — Our Helper in Prayer

The Holy Spirit is our divine Helper who intercedes through us. Romans 8:26–27 (NKJV) explains:

"Likewise, the Spirit also helps in our weaknesses. For we do not know what we should pray for as we ought,
but the Spirit Himself makes intercession for us with groanings which cannot be uttered.
Now He who searches the hearts knows what the mind of the Spirit is, because He makes intercession for the saints according to the will of God."

This means that when our words fail, the Spirit prays perfectly. He knows the Father's will and aligns our petitions accordingly. He turns sighs into intercession and tears into power.

When the Holy Spirit prays through us, every prayer becomes prophetic — birthed from heaven's heart, not human thought.

The Transformation at Pentecost

The outpouring of the Holy Spirit at Pentecost transformed fearful disciples into fearless witnesses and powerless prayers into fiery intercessors. Before Pentecost, Peter denied Christ before a servant girl. After Pentecost, he stood before multitudes and declared, "This Jesus God has raised up, of which we are all witnesses." (Acts 2:32, NKJV).

The difference was the power of the Holy Spirit. He turned weakness into boldness and silence into proclamation. The same Spirit who empowered them to speak with new tongues also empowered them to pray with divine authority.

The early Church was birthed in a prayer meeting — a collective outpouring of hearts seeking God. And through that, the world was changed forever.

Praying in the Spirit Today

The baptism of the Holy Spirit was not meant for one generation; it is the Father's gift to every believer who desires deeper fellowship and power in prayer.

Praying in the Spirit is not emotional expression — it is divine communication. It bypasses the mind and allows the Spirit to pray mysteries according to God's perfect will (1 Corinthians 14:2).

When believers pray in the Spirit:

- Faith increases — the inner man is strengthened.

- Revelation flows — the Spirit gives insight into God's Word and will.

- Bondage breaks — the presence of God fills the atmosphere.

- Unity grows — the same Spirit joins hearts together in worship and intercession.

This is why Paul encouraged believers, "Praying always with all prayer and supplication in the Spirit." (Ephesians 6:18, NKJV).

The Spirit of Prayer and Intercession

The Holy Spirit not only gives the language of prayer but also the burden of intercession. Isaiah 59:19 speaks of the "Spirit of the Lord lifting up a standard against the enemy." When the Spirit stirs a believer to pray, it is heaven's alarm — God using man to fulfill His will on earth.

Many revivals in history began when believers allowed the Spirit to intercede through them in groanings and tears. Such prayer carries heaven's urgency. It is not rehearsed but released. It is not planned but birthed by the Spirit.

When we yield fully to the Holy Spirit, prayer becomes partnership — the Spirit prays through us while we stand in agreement.

Walking in Continual Fellowship with the Spirit

To live a life of effective prayer, we must maintain fellowship with the Holy Spirit daily. He is the Counselor, Comforter, and constant Companion who teaches us how to commune with the Father.

2 Corinthians 13:14 (NKJV) says,

"The grace of the Lord Jesus Christ, and the love of God, and the communion of the Holy Spirit be with you all."

Communion means fellowship — sharing thoughts, desires, and affections. The more we walk with the Spirit, the more naturally prayer flows.

A Spirit-filled believer does not pray only when trouble comes; prayer becomes a constant rhythm of the heart — a life lived in fellowship with God.

Reflection and Prayer

Reflection :

The Holy Spirit empowers us to pray beyond our human understanding. Through His baptism and presence, we receive a heavenly language, divine strength, and perfect alignment with God's will. Pentecost marked not the end, but the beginning of Spirit-filled prayer that continues in the Church today.

Prayer:

Precious Holy Spirit, thank You for being my Helper and Intercessor. Baptize me afresh with Your power and fill me with Your presence. Teach me to pray in the Spirit with boldness and understanding. Let the fire that fell at Pentecost burn in me today. Empower my prayers to release Your will on earth and strengthen me to walk in continual fellowship with You. In Jesus' name, Amen.

Chapter Ten: Praying in the Name of Jesus

Every believer has been given a name greater than any other — a name that opens heaven, silences hell, and carries divine authority before the throne of God: the name of Jesus Christ. When we pray in His name, we are not using a closing phrase; we are exercising covenant power.

Praying in the name of Jesus is not a formality — it is a legal and spiritual declaration of access, authority, and relationship. It is through that name that we approach the Father, receive grace, and release divine power into earthly situations.

The Authority of the Name

Before His ascension, Jesus gave His disciples a revelation that would forever transform prayer. In John 14:13–14 (NKJV), He said:

"And whatever you ask in My name, that I will do, that the Father may be glorified in the Son.

If you ask anything in My name, I will do it."

This promise was not given to the world, but to His followers — those who abide in Him. The authority of Jesus' name rests on relationship and obedience. To pray in His name means to stand in His stead, to represent His will, and to speak with His authority.

When believers pray in the name of Jesus, heaven recognizes that name — the name that conquered sin, death, and the grave. Philippians 2:9–10 (NKJV) declares:

"Therefore, God also has highly exalted Him and given Him the name which is above every name,
that at the name of Jesus every knee should bow, of those in heaven, and of those on earth, and of those under the earth."

The name of Jesus is heaven's seal of authority on the prayers of the redeemed.

Praying in the Name of Jesus — More Than a Phrase

To pray "in Jesus' name" is more than saying the words at the end of a prayer. It means praying in alignment with His character, His purpose, and His will.

Jesus explained in John 15:7 (NKJV):

"If you abide in Me, and My words abide in you, you will ask what you desire, and it shall be done for you."

Abiding in Him means living in constant fellowship, obedience, and dependence. His name becomes powerful on our lips when His Word abides in our hearts.

Praying in His name is like carrying the signature of Christ on our requests. It tells heaven, "This prayer has been authorized by the Son of God."

The Finished Work of Christ — The Basis of Our Access

Before the cross, humanity approached God through the sacrifices of priests and animals. But through His death and resurrection, Jesus became our High Priest and Mediator. Hebrews 10:19–20 (NKJV) declares:

"Therefore, brethren, having boldness to enter the Holiest by the blood of Jesus,
by a new and living way which He consecrated for us, through the veil, that is, His flesh."

The blood of Jesus opened a permanent doorway into the presence of God. Now we no longer come as beggars but as sons and daughters with rightful access.

When we pray in His name, we are standing on the foundation of His finished work — the power of the cross and the victory of the resurrection. His name carries the weight of His sacrifice.

The Power of His Name in the Early Church

The early believers understood and demonstrated the authority in the name of Jesus. In Acts 3:6 (NKJV), Peter said to the lame man at the gate Beautiful,

"Silver and gold I do not have, but what I do have I give you: In the name of Jesus Christ of Nazareth, rise up and walk."

Immediately, the man leaped to his feet. Peter was not invoking a formula — he was exercising divine authority. Later, when questioned, Peter boldly declared,

"By the name of Jesus Christ of Nazareth, whom you crucified, whom God raised from the dead, by Him this man stands here before you whole." (Acts 4:10, NKJV).

The apostles prayed, preached, healed, and cast out demons in that name — and the world was turned upside down.

The same power is available today. Jesus said in Mark 16:17–18 (NKJV):

"And these signs will follow those who believe: In My name they will cast out demons; they will speak with new tongues.
they will lay hands on the sick, and they will recover."

When prayer is offered in His name, heaven acts because that name carries divine authority over sickness, sin, and every power of darkness.

The Conditions for Praying in His Name

For prayer in Jesus' name to be effective, certain conditions must be met:

1.   We must belong to Him.
The power of His name is given to those who are in covenant relationship through salvation.

   1.   We must believe in His authority.
        Faith gives power to the name we use. Acts 3:16 (NKJV) says, *"And His name, through faith in His name, has made this man strong."*

   2.   We must pray according to His will.
        1 John 5:14–15 (NKJV) affirms, *"If we ask anything according to His will, He hears us."*

   3.   We must glorify the Father.
        Jesus said, "That the Father may be glorified in the Son." (John 14:13).
        Every prayer in His name should bring glory to God, not self.

The Meaning of "In Jesus' Name"

Praying in Jesus' name means:

- I am standing on His righteousness, not my own.

- I am trusting in His power, not my strength.

- I am seeking His glory, not my recognition.

- I am surrendering to His will, not my desire.

It is the believer's declaration that "I come not in my name, but in the name of the One who died and rose again."

The Heavenly Recognition of His Name

When a believer prays in the name of Jesus, heaven responds immediately because that name is divine authority. Angels recognize it, demons tremble at it, and the Father honors it.

Jesus Himself assured in John 16:23–24 (NKJV):

"Most assuredly, I say to you, whatever you ask the Father in My name He will give you.
Until now you have asked nothing in My name. Ask, and you will receive, that your joy may be full."

The name of Jesus is not only the key to answered prayer but the source of abiding joy, because every answered prayer brings glory to Him.

The Responsibility of Bearing His Name

To use the name of Jesus is both a privilege and a responsibility. We must bear that name with purity, reverence, and faith. The seven sons of Sceva in Acts 19:13–16 attempted to use it without relationship or authority, and the evil spirit replied,

"Jesus I know, and Paul I know; but who are you?"

This story reminds us that power in the name of Jesus comes through relationship, not ritual. We must walk daily in obedience and fellowship with Him.

Reflection and Prayer

Reflection :

The name of Jesus gives us bold access to the Father and authority over every power of darkness. To pray in His name is to align with His will, depend on His power, and bring glory to His Father His name is our signature of victory and the key that unlocks heaven's storehouse.

Prayer:

Father, thank You for giving me access to Your presence through the name of Jesus. Teach me to honor that name with faith and purity. Let every prayer I make bring glory to You and advance Your kingdom. I stand in the power of Jesus' name over every challenge, sickness, and situation. I declare that at His name every knee must bow and every tongue confess that Jesus Christ is Lord. In His mighty name I pray, Amen.

CHAPTER ELEVEN:
PRAYER AND REVIVAL

Every revival, whether in Scripture or in history, can be traced back to one common root — prayer. Whenever God moves mightily upon the earth, He first stirs the hearts of His people to pray. Revival is not a spontaneous eruption; it is the divine response to hunger, repentance, and persistent intercession.

Prayer is the womb of revival. It births renewal in individuals, families, churches, and nations. Before the fire of revival falls publicly, it burns privately in the hearts of those who seek God earnestly.

The Nature of Revival

Revival is not merely an emotional stirring or a series of meetings—it is the reawakening of God's presence among His people. It brings life where there was dryness, passion where there was apathy, and holiness where there was compromise.

Psalm 85:6 (NKJV) captures the heart-cry of revival:

"Will You not revive us again, that Your people may rejoice in You?"

Revival begins when prayer becomes desperate—when believers cry, "Lord, we cannot live without You." It is a divine visitation that restores the fear of the Lord, renews faith, and ignites love for souls.

1. Revival in Nineveh — A City Saved by Prayer and Repentance

One of the most remarkable revivals recorded in Scripture occurred in the city of Nineveh. When Jonah finally obeyed God's command to preach repentance, the entire city—from the king to the least servant—believed the message and turned to God.

Jonah 3:5–10 (NKJV) says,

"So, the people of Nineveh believed God, proclaimed a fast, and put on sackcloth, from the greatest to the least of them… Then God saw their works, that they turned from their evil way; and God relented from the disaster that He had said He would bring upon them, and He did not do it."

Their repentance moved God's heart. Prayer and fasting turned judgment into mercy. What politics, culture, and religion could not change, prayer did in a single generation.

2. Revival in Israel Under Elijah — The Fire on Mount Carmel

During the days of Elijah, Israel had turned away from God, worshiping Baal. But through the prophet's prayer, God displayed His power.

1 Kings 18:36–37 (NKJV) records Elijah's prayer:

"Lord God of Abraham, Isaac, and Israel, let it be known this day that You are God in Israel and I am Your servant… Hear me, O Lord, hear me, that this people may know that You are the Lord God."

Immediately, fire fell from heaven and consumed the sacrifice. The people fell on their faces and cried, "The Lord, He is God!" Revival broke out because one man prayed with faith and zeal for God's glory.

Elijah's prayer was short, but it was sincere, faith-filled, and focused on God's honor—not his own. Revival always begins when God's glory becomes the object of our desire.

3. Revival in the Upper Room — Pentecost

The greatest revival of all began with prayer. In obedience to Jesus' command, the disciples gathered in Jerusalem and waited for the promise of the Father. Acts 1:14 (NKJV) says,

"These all continued with one accord in prayer and supplication."

They were united, persistent, and expectant. Their prayer birthed the Church.

Then, on the Day of Pentecost, heaven responded. Acts 2:1–4 (NKJV) declares,

"When the Day of Pentecost had fully come, they were all with one accord in one place.
And suddenly there came a sound from heaven, as of a rushing mighty wind...
And they were all filled with the Holy Spirit and began to speak with other tongues, as the Spirit gave them utterance."

The fire of God fell again, this time not on an altar of stone, but upon the hearts of men. From that moment, the world was never the same. Three thousand souls were saved that very day.

Pentecost shows that when believers unite in prayer, the heavens open, and the Holy Spirit descends with power.

4. Revival in the Early Church

After Pentecost, prayer remained the heartbeat of the early Church. Acts 2:42 (NKJV) says,

"And they continued steadfastly in the apostles' doctrine and fellowship, in the breaking of bread, and in prayers."

Because of their devotion to prayer, miracles became normal. The sick were healed, the dead were raised, and the gospel spread like wildfire. When persecution arose, they did not hide—they prayed for boldness. Acts 4:31 (NKJV) records,

"And when they had prayed, the place where they were assembled together was shaken; and they were all filled with the Holy Spirit, and they spoke the word of God with boldness."

Revival was sustained because prayer never ceased. They understood that prayer is the engine of the Church.

5. Personal Revival Begins in the Heart

Revival is not only for nations—it begins within us. When the believer's heart grows cold, prayer rekindles the flame. When worship becomes routine, prayer restores passion.

Psalm 51:10–12 (NKJV) is David's personal revival prayer:

*"Create in me a clean heart, O God, and renew a steadfast spirit within me.
Do not cast me away from Your presence, and do not take Your Holy Spirit from me.
Restore to me the joy of Your salvation, and uphold me by Your generous Spirit."*

Revival begins when we allow the Spirit of God to reignite our love for Him and renew our desire for holiness.

6. Historical Glimpses of Revival Through Prayer

Throughout church history, every awakening was born in the secret place:

- The Moravian Revival (1727): Began with a small prayer meeting in Herrnhut, Germany. The prayer continued non-stop, day and night, for over 100 years.

- The Welsh Revival (1904): Sparked through the prayers of a young man named Evan Roberts, who cried, "Bend me, O Lord!" Within months, over 100,000 people came to Christ.

- The Azusa Street Revival (1906): Began in a humble prayer meeting in Los Angeles led by William Seymour. The power of the Holy Spirit was poured out, and the modern Pentecostal movement was born.

Each revival began not with crowds, but with kneeling saints whose prayers touched heaven and changed the world.

7. The Keys to Revival Prayer

1. Repentance: Revival begins with brokenness over sin.

- *"If My people who are called by My name will humble themselves, and pray and seek My face, and turn from their wicked ways..." (2 Chronicles 7:14, NKJV).*

2. Unity: Division quenches the Spirit; unity invites Him.

- *"They were all with one accord in one place." (Acts 2:1, NKJV).*

3. Faith: Believing that God is able to revive.

- *"All things are possible to him who believes." (Mark 9:23, NKJV).*

4. Persistence: Refusing to give up until God moves.

- *Elijah prayed seven times for rain. Daniel prayed twenty-one days for understanding.*

5. Desire for God's Glory: Revival comes when we seek God Himself, not just His blessings.

The Fruit of Revival

When revival comes, everything changes:

- Sinners are saved.

- The Church is purified.

- Love and holiness increase.

- Miracles and spiritual gifts manifest.

- The fear of God fills hearts.

- Society begins to transform.

True revival is not man's achievement—it is God's visitation.

Reflection and Prayer

Reflection :

Revival is born in prayer, sustained by prayer, and revealed through prayer. When the people of God humble themselves and cry out for His presence, heaven responds with power. Every revival begins in the secret place — on the knees of those who hunger for God's glory.

Prayer:

Father, revive my heart and renew my love for You. Pour out Your Spirit once again upon Your Church and upon the nations. Stir us to pray until Your presence fills our lives, our homes, and our cities. Let the fire that fell at Pentecost burn anew in our generation. Awaken the sleeping hearts, heal the backslidden, and ignite holy passion for Your kingdom. Lord, let revival begin in me today. In Jesus' name, Amen.

66

Chapter Twelve:
The Ultimate Prayer: "Thy Will Be Done"

Every believer who grows in prayer eventually comes to a sacred place — the place of surrender. It is the point where prayer ceases to be about what we want and becomes about what God desires. The highest form of prayer is not petition, intercession, or even thanksgiving; it is yielding to the will of the Father.

This is the prayer that brings rest to the soul, peace to the mind, and power to the spirit. It is the prayer Jesus prayed in the most difficult hour of His life:

"Not My will, but Yours, be done." (Luke 22:42, NKJV)

These few words carry the weight of heaven's greatest victory.

The Scene in Gethsemane

The night before His crucifixion, Jesus went with His disciples to the Garden of Gethsemane — a place He often visited to pray. The name Gethsemane means "oil press," symbolizing crushing and yielding. It was there that the Son of God faced the greatest test of obedience.

Matthew 26:36–39 (NKJV) records:

"Then Jesus came with them to a place called Gethsemane, and said to the disciples, 'Sit here while I go and pray over there.'
And He took with Him Peter and the two sons of Zebedee, and He began to be sorrowful and deeply distressed.
Then He said to them, 'My soul is exceedingly sorrowful, even to death. Stay here and watch with Me.'
He went a little farther and fell on His face, and prayed, saying, 'O My Father, if it is possible, let this cup pass from Me; nevertheless, not as I will, but as You will.'"

In that prayer, we see the full humanity and divinity of Jesus. He felt the weight of sin, sorrow, and the cross, yet He chose submission over self. He yielded His will to the Father's perfect plan.

Surrender — The Highest Form of Prayer

The prayer of surrender is not weakness — it is power under control. It is the heart saying, "Lord, I trust You, even when I don't understand You."

Jesus did not pray to escape the cross; He prayed for strength to fulfill the Father's purpose. His surrender turned suffering into salvation, defeat into victory, and death into eternal life.

When we pray, "Thy will be done," we align ourselves with divine wisdom that sees beyond our limited understanding. God's will is not always easy, but it is always perfect.

Romans 12:2 (NKJV) reminds us:

"Do not be conformed to this world, but be transformed by the renewing of your mind, that you may prove what is that good and acceptable and perfect will of God."

Surrender is transformation. It changes how we see, think, and pray.

The Struggle of the Will

Even the Son of God faced the agony of surrender. Luke 22:44 (NKJV) says,

"And being in agony, He prayed more earnestly. Then His sweat became like great drops of blood falling down to the ground."

That was not a moment of weakness, but of warfare. The battle was not against soldiers or Satan — it was between the human will and the divine plan. And Jesus won through prayer.

We, too, face moments when our desires, dreams, or timing clash with God's plan. In those moments, the true test of maturity is our willingness to say, "Not my will, but Yours be done."

Every surrendered prayer is a seed that bears eternal fruit.

The Answer to Jesus' Prayer

At first glance, it may seem that God did not answer Jesus' plea for the cup to pass. Yet the Father did answer — not by removing the cup, but by sending strength. Luke 22:43 (NKJV) tells us,

"Then an angel appeared to Him from heaven, strengthening Him."

God's answer to surrendered prayer is often strength, not escape. When we yield to His will, we receive divine enabling to endure and overcome.

The ultimate proof of love is obedience, and the ultimate expression of obedience is surrender.

The Will of God — The Anchor of Faith

True faith does not demand its own way. It trusts God's wisdom even when His path leads through valleys and shadows. Faith is not insisting, "Lord, do it my way," but believing, "Lord, You know the best way."

1 John 5:14 (NKJV) declares:

"Now this is the confidence that we have in Him, that if we ask anything according to His will, He hears us."

The assurance of answered prayer rests in this — that His will is always better than ours. The peace that follows surrender is greater than any answer we could demand.

Biblical Examples of Surrendered Prayer

- Abraham yielded his will when he offered Isaac on the altar (Genesis 22). His obedience opened the door for God's covenant blessing.

- Mary, the mother of Jesus, said, "Let it be to me according to your word." (Luke 1:38, NKJV). Her surrender brought forth the Savior of the world.

- Paul prayed three times for the thorn in his flesh to be removed, but God replied, "My grace is sufficient for you." (2 Corinthians 12:9, NKJV). Paul's surrender turned weakness into strength.

Each of these examples reveals that the greatest victories come through yielded hearts.

The Reward of Surrender

When we yield to God's will, several things happen:

1. Peace replaces anxiety. (Philippians 4:6–7)

2.   God's strength sustains us. (Isaiah 40:31)

3.   His purpose is fulfilled in us. (Romans 8:28)

4.   Our faith matures. (James 1:3–4)

Surrender brings us into harmony with heaven. It teaches us that God's delays are not denials, and His ways, though mysterious, always lead to glory.

Living the Prayer of Surrender

To live "Thy will be done" is to walk daily in trust and obedience. It means:

- Choosing faith over fear.

- Submitting our plans to His timing.

- Allowing God to write the story of our lives without resisting His pen.

This posture keeps us in perfect peace, for Isaiah 26:3 (NKJV) says,

"You will keep him in perfect peace, whose mind is stayed on You, because he trusts in You."

The heart that surrenders finds strength even in storms because it knows the One who commands the wind and the waves.

Reflection and Prayer

Reflection :

The ultimate prayer is surrender — trusting God's will above our own. When we yield, we do not lose; we gain divine strength, peace, and victory. In Gethsemane, Jesus showed that submission is not defeat, but triumph through obedience.

Prayer:

Father, I surrender my will, desires, and plans to You. Teach me to trust Your wisdom above my understanding. Even when I cannot see the full picture, help me rest in Your perfect will. Strengthen me to obey You, even when obedience costs me everything. Let my life echo the words of Jesus: "Not my will, but Yours be done." May Your purpose be fulfilled in me and through me. In Jesus' name, Amen.

Chapter Thirteen:
The Results and Rewards of Prayer

Prayer is never in vain. Every sincere prayer sown in faith bears fruit, whether seen immediately or in due season. When a believer prays, something always happens — in the heart, in the heavens, and in the world around them.

God hears, God moves, and God answers according to His will. He never ignores the cry of the righteous. Psalm 34:15 (NKJV) assures us,

"The eyes of the Lord are on the righteous, and His ears are open to their cry."

The results of prayer are both spiritual and practical. Prayer not only brings change to circumstances; it also changes us — shaping our character, renewing our minds, and deepening our relationship with the Father.

1. Prayer Brings the Presence of God

The first and greatest reward of prayer is not an answered request, but God Himself. True prayer ushers us into His presence, where joy, strength, and revelation overflow.

Psalm 16:11 (NKJV) declares,

"In Your presence is fullness of joy; at Your right hand are pleasures forevermore."

When we pray, we enter that presence. Prayer is the meeting place of divine fellowship — the sacred space where the Creator communes with His creation.

Moses understood this. He prayed, "If Your Presence does not go with us, do not bring us up from here." (Exodus 33:15, NKJV). He valued God's presence above any promise.

In prayer, we are not only heard — we are embraced. His presence becomes our peace, and His nearness our greatest treasure.

2. Prayer Brings Answers and Breakthroughs

Jesus taught plainly that prayer moves the hand of God. In Matthew 7:7 (NKJV), He said,

"Ask, and it will be given to you; seek, and you will find; knock, and it will be opened to you."

Prayer opens doors that no man can shut. It calls forth divine provision and aligns situations with heaven's order.

- Elijah prayed, and rain returned to the land.

- Hannah prayed, and a prophet was born.

- Daniel prayed, and angelic revelation came.

- The early Church prayed, and prison doors opened.

God delights to answer prayers that honor His will. Jeremiah 33:3 (NKJV) declares,

"Call to Me, and I will answer you, and show you great and mighty things, which you do not know."

When prayer becomes the believer's habit, miracles become the believer's expectation.

3. Prayer Brings Peace Beyond Understanding

One of the sweetest rewards of prayer is peace — a calm assurance that guards the heart even before the answer arrives.

Philippians 4:6–7 (NKJV) teaches:

"Be anxious for nothing, but in everything by prayer and supplication, with thanksgiving, let your requests be made known to God.
and the peace of God, which surpasses all understanding, will guard your hearts and minds through Christ Jesus."

This peace is not the absence of trouble; it is the presence of God in the midst of it. It silences fear, stabilizes faith, and strengthens hope.

The one who prays continually learns to rest, knowing that God is in control.

4. Prayer Produces Spiritual Strength and Endurance

Prayer strengthens the spirit just as exercise strengthens the body. It renews spiritual stamina and sharpens discernment. Isaiah 40:31 (NKJV) says,

"But those who wait on the Lord shall renew their strength; they shall mount up with wings like eagles, they shall run and not be weary, they shall walk and not faint."

Every time you pray, strength from heaven flows into your soul. Jesus, after long hours of ministry, often withdrew to pray — not because He was weak, but because He drew strength from fellowship with the Father.

When we spend time in prayer, we exchange our weakness for God's strength. That is why people who pray much endure much.

5. Prayer Builds Intimacy and Friendship with God

Prayer deepens our relationship with God until He is no longer distant but intimately known. Abraham was called "the friend of God" (James 2:23) because he communed with Him continually.

True friendship with God is built in prayer — in honest, daily fellowship. As we pour out our hearts before Him, we begin to understand His heart.

John 15:15 (NKJV) reveals Jesus' desire for intimacy:

"No longer do I call you servants... but I have called you friends, for all things that I heard from My Father I have made known to you."

Prayer transforms servants into friends. It is in the quiet place that God reveals His secrets to those who love Him.

6. Prayer Releases Divine Direction and Wisdom

One of the greatest results of prayer is clarity. When we pray, confusion gives way to divine direction. God delights to guide those who seek Him.

Proverbs 3:6 (NKJV) says,

"In all your ways acknowledge Him, and He shall direct your paths."

Through prayer, the Holy Spirit whispers wisdom into the heart. Decisions become clear, and steps become sure.

David often inquired of the Lord before going into battle, and God gave him specific instructions for victory (1 Samuel 30:8). Likewise, believers who make prayer their first response never lack guidance.

7. Prayer Releases Power and Authority

Prayer releases heaven's authority on earth. Jesus gave His disciples power over all the works of the enemy, but that authority operates through prayer.

Luke 10:19 (NKJV) says,

"Behold, I give you the authority to trample on serpents and scorpions, and over all the power of the enemy, and nothing shall by any means hurt you."

The early Church prayed and saw demons flee, chains break, and the sick healed. That same authority still works through prayer today. When a believer prays in faith, the spiritual atmosphere shifts, and the kingdom of darkness loses ground.

8. Prayer Brings Transformation of the Heart

The most profound result of prayer is the transformation it brings within. Prayer changes the one who prays. It molds character, softens pride, and births compassion.

As we behold God in prayer, we are changed into His image. 2 Corinthians 3:18 (NKJV) says,

"But we all, with unveiled face, beholding as in a mirror the glory of the Lord, are being transformed into the same image from glory to glory."

Prayer is not only about receiving from God but becoming like Him. Every time we pray, His presence reshapes us into vessels of grace and holiness.

9. Prayer Opens Doors of Revival and Blessing

Prayer precedes revival, and revival brings blessing. When believers unite in prayer, heaven responds with rain upon the dry ground.

Zechariah 10:1 (NKJV) declares,

"Ask the Lord for rain in the time of the latter rain. The Lord will make flashing clouds; He will give them showers of rain, grass in the field for everyone."

Every outpouring of the Spirit begins with asking. The more we pray, the more heaven pours. Prayer prepares the soil for revival and the harvest of souls.

10. The Eternal Reward of Prayer

Prayer not only blesses us in this life but also carries eternal reward. Revelation 5:8 (NKJV) describes the prayers of the saints as

"golden bowls full of incense, which are the prayers of the saints."

Every prayer offered in faith is remembered before God. Even those whispered in tears are stored in heaven and will one day be revealed as part of God's eternal story.

No prayer prayed in faith is ever forgotten.

Reflection and Prayer

Reflection :

Prayer brings the greatest of all rewards — the presence of God, the peace of Christ, and the power of the Holy Spirit. It opens heaven, transforms hearts, and fulfills God's will on earth. Every moment spent in prayer is a step deeper into God's heart and a seed that will bear eternal fruit.

Prayer:

Father, thank You for the power and privilege of prayer. Thank You that You hear, answer, and transform through every prayer offered in faith. Fill my heart with unceasing gratitude for the peace, strength, and presence that prayer brings. Help me to live a life that depends on You completely and to rejoice in every answer You give. Let my life testify that prayer profoundly changes things — because prayer changes me In Jesus' name, Amen.

Chapter Fourteen: The Call to a Life of Prayer

Prayer was never meant to be occasional; it was designed to be continual. It is not only what we do — it is who we are as children of God. The true believer is not identified by how often they attend church or how eloquently they speak, but by the depth of their communion with God in prayer.

Prayer is the breath of the soul, the heartbeat of faith, and the oxygen of spiritual life. To stop praying is to suffocate spiritually; to live in prayer is to live in the power and presence of God.

A Life Built on Communion

The Lord never intended for prayer to be a distant duty. It is meant to be a daily delight — a constant conversation between heaven and earth.

Paul wrote in 1 Thessalonians 5 :17 (NKJV) :

"Pray without ceasing."

That does not mean being on our knees every minute but walking through each moment with a prayerful heart — conscious of God's nearness, aware of His voice, and yielded to His will.

Jesus lived this way. Though He often withdrew to pray in solitude, His heart remained in continual fellowship with the Father. He prayed when healing the sick, when feeding the multitudes, when giving thanks, and even when facing the cross. His life was prayer in motion.

The more we walk with God, the more prayer becomes natural. It ceases to be an event and becomes a lifestyle.

The Secret Place: Where Relationship Is Kept Alive

Every believer needs a "secret place" — a consistent meeting ground with God. Jesus taught in Matthew 6:6 (NKJV):

"But you, when you pray, go into your room, and when you have shut your door, pray to your Father who is in the secret place; and your Father who sees in secret will reward you openly."

The secret place is where intimacy is built and where power is born. It's where we pour out our hearts, receive divine counsel, and are renewed in His presence.

Every revival in the soul begins in that place. A prayerless Christian is a powerless Christian, but a prayerful Christian becomes unstoppable.

Prayer as Relationship, Not Ritual

Religion prays out of obligation; relationship prays out of love. When prayer becomes a routine instead of a relationship, it loses its life and power.

The psalmist said, "O God, You are my God; early will I seek You; my soul thirsts for You." (Psalm 63:1, NKJV). That is the heartbeat of a praying life — desire.

When prayer flows from love rather than duty, it becomes joy. And when love fuels prayer, it never grows cold.

The Holy Spirit — Our Constant Companion

The Holy Spirit makes continual prayer possible. He dwells within us as our Helper, teaching us to pray even when words fail. Romans 8:26 (NKJV) says:

"Likewise the Spirit also helps in our weaknesses... the Spirit Himself makes intercession for us with groanings which cannot be uttered."

He leads, guides, and reminds us of the Father's will. Through the Spirit, prayer becomes an unbroken conversation — a flow of grace, worship, and intercession that never ceases.

To live a life of prayer is to live a Spirit-filled life.

The Example of Jesus — Our Pattern of Prayer

Jesus modeled what a life of prayer looks like. He prayed before dawn (Mark 1:35), before choosing the twelve disciples (Luke 6:12), before raising Lazarus (John 11:41), and in His greatest agony at Gethsemane (Luke 22:44).

He prayed for others (John 17), for forgiveness (Luke 23:34), and even for those who crucified Him. His every act was saturated in prayer.

To follow Christ is to follow His pattern of prayer. If the Son of God needed to pray, how much more must we?

The Power of a Consistent Prayer Life

Consistency in prayer produces stability in faith. A life of prayer builds endurance against temptation, wisdom in decision-making, and peace in trials.

Daniel prayed three times a day, even when threatened with death. His consistency brought divine favor and protection. The early Church "continued steadfastly" in prayer and experienced daily miracles. (Acts 2:42–47).

Consistency transforms prayer from an event into a lifestyle and from a habit into a heartbeat.

Prayer Keeps the Fire Burning

In the Old Testament, the priests were commanded to keep the altar fire burning continually. Leviticus 6:13 (NKJV) says,

"A fire shall always be burning on the altar; it shall never go out."

Today, that altar is our heart. Prayer keeps the flame alive. When prayer ceases, the fire dims; when prayer abounds, the fire blazes.

Revival in the Church and power in the believer depend on this unquenchable flame of continual prayer.

Prayer as Partnership With God

Prayer is not merely communication — it is cooperation with heaven. Through prayer, God invites us to participate in His work on earth.

Jesus said, "Whatever you bind on earth will be bound in heaven, and whatever you loose on earth will be loosed in heaven." (Matthew 18:18, NKJV).

The praying believer becomes a partner with God in shaping destinies, releasing healing, breaking strongholds, and advancing His kingdom.

To live a life of prayer is to live as an agent of heaven on earth.

The Rewards of a Prayerful Life

Those who walk in continual prayer experience:

1.   Deeper intimacy with God.

2.   Greater peace and strength in trials.

3.   Clearer direction and discernment.

4.   Increased spiritual authority.

5.   Unshakable faith in every season.

Psalm 91 :1 (NKJV) promises,

"He who dwells in the secret place of the Most High shall abide under the shadow of the Almighty."

The prayerful life is a life lived under divine covering.

A Call to the Church and Every Believer

The Spirit of God is calling His people back to the altar — to the life of prayer that sustains revival, purity, and power. The time for shallow Christianity is over. The hour is late, and the need for intercessors is urgent.

Ezekiel 22:30 (NKJV) records God's cry :

"So I sought for a man among them who would make a wall, and stand in the gap before Me on behalf of the land... but I found no one."

Let it not be said of our generation that God found no one. Let every believer answer the call: "Here I am, Lord — teach me to pray."

Reflection and Prayer

Reflection :

A life of prayer is a life of power, peace, and purpose. God is calling His Church back to intimacy, not merely activity — to communion, not just communication. Prayer changes things because prayer changes us.

Prayer:

Heavenly Father, thank You for calling me to a life of prayer. Teach me to walk with You daily, to listen to Your voice, and to dwell continually in Your presence. Let prayer be my joy, my strength, and my constant fellowship with You. Revive in me a hunger to seek Your face, to intercede for others, and to live as a vessel of Your presence. Keep the fire on my altar burning day and night until I see You face to face. In Jesus' name, Amen.

FINAL PRAYER AND CONCLUSION

Conclusion: Living a Life That Moves the Hand of God

Prayer has always been the meeting place between heaven and earth — the bridge that connects human weakness to divine power. Through prayer, ordinary men and women have done extraordinary things because they touched the heart of the Almighty.

From Abraham who interceded for Sodom, to Moses who stood in the gap for Israel; from Hannah who wept for a son, to Elijah who called down fire; from Daniel who prayed until angels moved, to Jesus who prayed until His sweat became as drops of blood — the testimony is the same: Prayer changes things.

But more than circumstances, prayer changes people. It purifies motives, molds character, renews strength, and draws the believer closer to the presence of God. When prayer becomes a way of life, it transforms how we think, love, forgive, and live.

The call to prayer is the call to intimacy. It is an invitation to walk with God daily — not from a distance, but in the warmth of His fellowship. When the heart learns to pray, it learns to love, to trust, and to surrender. Prayer births revival in the soul before it awakens the world.

In every generation, God looks for men and women who will stand before Him in prayer — those who will carry His burden, intercede for others, and release His will on the earth. You are part of that calling.

Let prayer no longer be the last resort, but the first response. Let it not be a moment of desperation, but a lifestyle of devotion.

As you close this book, may you open your heart anew to the Spirit of God who empowers and teaches you to pray. May you find joy in His presence, power in His promises, and peace in His will.

Remember: the strength of your walk with God will always mirror the depth of your prayer life. And when your heart aligns with His, even the impossible will bow.

"The effective, fervent prayer of a righteous man avails much."
(James 5:16, NKJV)

Final Prayer

Father of mercy and grace,

I thank You for the gift of prayer — the sacred privilege of communion with You. Thank You for every truth revealed through these pages, and for the invitation to draw nearer to Your heart.

Lord, teach me to pray with faith, humility, and persistence. Let my prayers rise before You as incense and let my heart remain steadfast in love and obedience. Help me to live in constant fellowship with You, to listen when You speak, and to follow wherever You lead.

Baptize me afresh with the Holy Spirit and with fire. Stir my soul to intercede for my family, my nation, and the Church. Let revival begin in me — let Your will be done through me.

Father, when words fail, let my spirit still commune with You. When storms arise, let prayer be my anchor. When blessings come, let prayer be my gratitude. May my life be a testimony that indeed, prayer changes things — because prayer changes me.

I surrender all to You, Lord. Let Your kingdom come, and let Your will be done on earth as it is in heaven.

In the mighty and precious name of Jesus Christ,

Amen.

9 781972 299456